TANZANIA

...in Pictures

Independent Picture Service

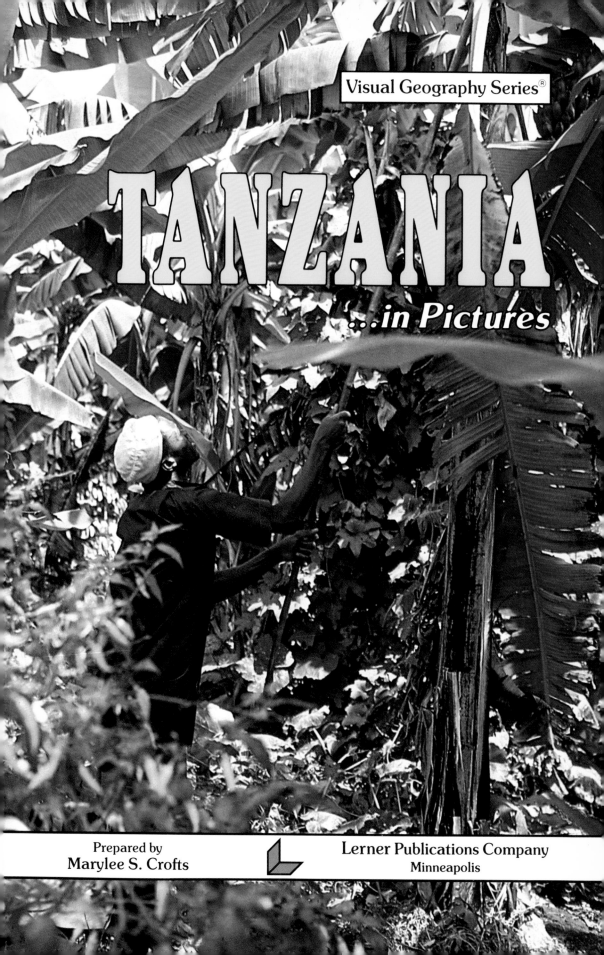

Visual Geography Series®

TANZANIA

...in Pictures

Prepared by
Marylee S. Crofts

Lerner Publications Company
Minneapolis

Independent Picture Service

To make copra, one of Zanzibar's chief exports, coconuts are cut in half, drained of their milk, and laid in the sun to dry.

This is an all-new edition of the Visual Geography Series. Previous editions have been published by Sterling Publishing Company, New York City, and some of the original textual information has been retained. New photographs, maps, charts, captions, and updated information have been added. The text has been entirely reset in 10/12 Century Textbook.

LIBRARY OF CONGRESS CATALOGING-IN-PUBLICATION DATA

Crofts, Marylee S.
    Tanzania in pictures / prepared by Marylee S. Crofts.
    p. cm.—(Visual geography series)
    Rev. ed. of: Tanzania in pictures / by Joel Reuben and
Howard Carstens.
    Includes index.
    Summary: An introduction to the geography, history, government, economy, culture, and people of the African country boasting that continent's highest mountain, deepest lake, and largest game reserve.
    ISBN 0-8225-1838-4 (lib. bdg.)
    1. Tanzania. [1. Tanzania.] I. Reuben, Joel. Tanzania in pictures. II. Lerner Publications Company. III. Title. IV. Series: Visual geography series (Minneapolis, Minn.)
DT438.C76 1988   87-26477
967.8'104—dc19   CIP
                                                   AC

International Standard Book Number: 0-8225-1838-4
Library of Congress Catalog Card Number: 87-26477

VISUAL GEOGRAPHY SERIES®

Publisher
Harry Jonas Lerner
Associate Publisher
Nancy M. Campbell
Senior Editor
Mary M. Rodgers
Editor
Gretchen Bratvold
Assistant Editors
Dan Filbin
Kathleen S. Heidel
Illustrations Editor
Karen A. Sirvaitis
Consultants/Contributors
Marylee S. Crofts
Sandra K. Davis
Designer
Jim Simondet
Cartographer
Carol F. Barrett
Indexer
Sylvia Timian
Production Manager
Richard J. Hannah

Independent Picture Service

Mountaineers climb Kibo, Mount Kilimanjaro's highest peak.

Acknowledgments

Title page photo by Phil Porter.

Elevation contours adapted from *The Times Atlas of the World,* seventh comprehensive edition (New York: Times Books, 1985).

1 2 3 4 5 6 7 8 9 10 97 96 95 94 93 92 91 90 89 88

Shoppers at a market near Arusha carry their goods in baskets made of sisal, a strong natural fiber.

Independent Picture Service

Contents

TANZANIA

N ↑

—— Province Boundaries

| 0 | 100 | 200 Miles |
| 0 | 100 | 200 Kilometers |

UGANDA

Lake Victoria

UKEREWE ISLAND

KENYA

Mara R.

SERENGETI NAT. PARK

Mbalangeti R.

RWANDA

Lake Natron

BURUNDI

Moyowosi R.

Mwanza

Mwadui

Shinyanga

Lake Eyasi

Arusha

Lake Manyara

Kondoa

Pangani R.

Tanga Railway

Tanga

PEMBA IS.

Wala Sagasi R.

Tabora

Lake Sagara

Central Railway

DODOMA

ZANZIBAR IS.

Zanzibar City

Bagamoyo

Dar es Salaam

Morogoro

ZAIRE

Lake Tanganyika

Lake Rukwa

KALAMBO FALLS

MAFIA IS.

Rufiji R.

Kilwa

INDIAN OCEAN

ZAMBIA

Lake Malawi

MALAWI

Ruvuma R.

MOZAMBIQUE

TANZANIA

AFRICA

20°

20°

EQUATOR

0°

SOUTH ATLANTIC OCEAN

INDIAN OCEAN

20°

| 0 | 1000 Miles |
| 0 | 1000 Kilometers |

METRIC CONVERSION CHART
To Find Approximate Equivalents

WHEN YOU KNOW:	MULTIPLY BY:	TO FIND:
AREA		
acres	0.41	hectares
square miles	2.59	square kilometers
CAPACITY		
gallons	3.79	liters
LENGTH		
feet	30.48	centimeters
yards	0.91	meters
miles	1.61	kilometers
MASS (weight)		
pounds	0.45	kilograms
tons	0.91	metric tons
VOLUME		
cubic yards	0.77	cubic meters
TEMPERATURE		
degrees Fahrenheit	0.56 (*after* subtracting 32)	degrees Celsius

A girl carries a load of dried sisal to balers.

Introduction

Tanzania was established when two newly independent nations, Tanganyika and Zanzibar, united in 1964. Parts of each country's name were combined to form the name of the new nation. Located on the African mainland, Tanganyika is in the region known as East Africa. Lying just off the coast of Tanganyika, Zanzibar is composed of several islands that took their national name from the largest and most prominent island. When Tanzania was formed, an era of common identity between the two countries began.

Before they became independent nations in the twentieth century, these regions experienced the domination of colonial powers. By the thirteenth century, Arab traders had developed Zanzibar into a major Indian Ocean port. The natural resources for their trade, including human beings who were sold as slaves, often came from the mainland region.

When Europeans explored the East African coast, the forerunners of today's Tanzanians encountered people from Portugal, Germany, and Great Britain. British colonial agents gained control of both regions by the twentieth century. By the 1950s Africans of each region were trying to gain national independence.

7

President Nyerere *(right)* was welcomed to the United Nations in 1963 by U Thant, who was secretary general of the United Nations at the time.

After winning the struggle for nationhood, Tanganyika and Zanzibar united to face the problems of economic survival and governmental instability. Tanzania is the largest and the poorest country in East Africa. Under the guidance of Julius Nyerere, a schoolteacher who became the nation's founder, Tanzania became nonaligned, that is, it maintains a neutral political stance toward the East and the West. The nation has welcomed economic assistance from the People's Republic of China, the Soviet Union, the United States, Great Britain, and others.

Tanzania's strong African identity was clearly established when the nation chose Kiswahili (also known as Swahili) as the national language. Despite the instability of the region, Tanzania pursues its motto, *Uhuru na Umoja,* which means "Freedom and Unity."

A fishery nestled on Tanzania's coast brings in enough fish to help supplement the diets of the area's residents.

Photo by Phil Porter

Ngorongoro Crater is the year-round home to millions of birds and to hundreds of thousands of animals, including this zebra and her offspring.

1) The Land

Larger than the states of Texas and Oklahoma combined, the United Republic of Tanzania is located on the east coast of Africa, just below the equator. The mainland, previously called Tanganyika, is nearly 362,500 square miles in area. The offshore portions of the nation are the Indian Ocean islands of Zanzibar, Pemba, Mafia, and other small, scattered islands.

Topography

Tanzania shares borders with Kenya and Uganda to the north; Rwanda, Burundi, and Zaire to the west; and Zambia, Malawi, and Mozambique to the south. The mainland's eastern boundary is the Indian Ocean, which has provided an important means of communication and transportation for Tanzania through the centuries.

THE MAINLAND

The islands and the coastal plain of the mainland are composed largely of coral —the accumulated skeletons of tiny sea animals. The 500-mile-long coastline is somewhat dangerous for ships to approach because of its many coral reefs and sandbars. The mainland rises from the coast as a large, rolling plain. The Great Rift Valley breaks up the expanse into several regions.

Extending for thousands of miles, the Great Rift Valley runs from southwestern Asia through the eastern length of Africa. Caused by violent movements in the earth's crust—the result of volcanic eruptions or earthquakes—the Great Rift Valley is a series of faultlines, called rifts.

In Tanzania the Great Rift Valley and its branch, the Western Rift Valley, helped to form large lakes, volcanic areas, and

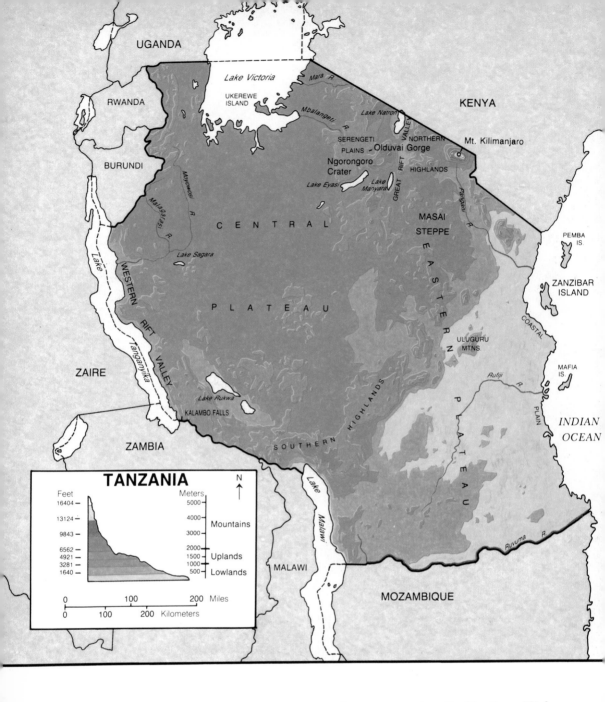

mountains. These rifts have divided Tanzania's plain into several plateaus and highland regions.

The country's coastal plain averages 20 miles in width. It rises sharply to about 3,500 feet above sea level to meet the Eastern Plateau, which is a general name for two distinct sections of eastern Tanzania.

In the upper section, the Northern Highlands contain Mount Kilimanjaro—the African continent's highest point at 19,340 feet. The Serengeti Plain is just to the west of this highland area. The Masai Steppe in northern Tanzania is one of the most dominant features of the Eastern Plateau. This large, arid terrain supports dry bushes and grass.

10

The dried grassland of Iringa province typifies vegetation in the Eastern Plateau.

Mount Kilimanjaro stands 3 degrees south of the equator.

Kalambo Falls flow from a short river into the southern part of Lake Tanganyika.

The Uluguru Mountains mark off the northern peak of the roughly triangular lower section of the Eastern Plateau. The base of the triangle runs from Lake Malawi in the west all the way east to Tanzania's coast. Isolated hills and rock outcroppings are found on the coastal side of the triangle. Near Lake Malawi, moun-

tains and grasslands—collectively called the Southern Highlands—characterize the landscape.

Between the Great Rift Valley and the Western Rift Valley lies the Central Plateau. This large plateau, at an elevation of 3,000 to 5,000 feet, is semi-arid and supports only low-level vegetation.

Tanzania is bordered by two extraordinary inland bodies of water. These are formed within the Western Rift Valley and are very deep, relatively narrow lakes. Lake Tanganyika lies partially within Tanzanian territory, marking the country's western border. The lake's floor is the deepest point on the African continent. Lake Malawi lies within the national territory of Malawi but forms part of Tanzania's southwestern border.

THE ISLANDS

Zanzibar Island lies 22 miles off Tanzania's mainland. From north to south, it is 50 miles long and measures 25 miles at its widest point. Like the several smaller islands—Pemba and Mafia, for example—that are part of Tanzania, Zanzibar is composed of coral. The western part of Zanzibar is hilly and slowly descends into a plain. The other islands lie a few miles farther off the mainland coast. Pemba is a steep, hilly island just a few miles north of Zanzibar, and Mafia is a low island about 100 miles to the south.

Lakes and Rivers

By volume, Lake Tanganyika is the third largest freshwater lake in the world. Because the Great Rift's mountainous walls hold Lake Tanganyika high above sea level, the lake only reaches 2,300 feet below sea level, although its overall depth is 4,730 feet.

In the north, Lake Victoria is divided between Tanzania, Uganda, and Kenya. Popularly known as the source of the Nile River, the lake stands at an elevation of 3,700 feet above sea level because it is

During the dry season, elephants kill many baobab trees by pulling down the branches to eat the leaves that remain at the top.

Courtesy of Minneapolis Public Library and Information Center

gathered between the branches of the Great and Western rifts. It is quite shallow, however, reaching only 270 feet in depth. Covering 26,828 square miles, Lake Victoria is the second largest freshwater lake by area in the world, second only to Lake Superior in North America.

The Nile, the longest river in the world, flows north from Lake Victoria, traveling through Uganda, Sudan, and Egypt before emptying into the Mediterranean Sea. Lake Tanganyika receives several western Tanzanian rivers—such as the Malagarasi and its tributary the Moyowosi—whose waters eventually find their way to the Atlantic Ocean on the western side of the continent. Rivers that flow eastward to the Indian Ocean—the Rufiji, the Pangani, and the Ruvuma, for example—provide irrigation and hydroelectric power for Tanzania.

Rainfall and Climate

Seasonal winds blow heavy rains from the northeast between October and February and from the southwest during the rest of the year. December is the rainiest month in most of the country, but, in the northeast and along the coast, a second rainy season begins in March or April. Rainfall in Tanzania ranges from over 40 inches per year along the coast and around Lake Victoria to 10 inches per year in the Central Plateau.

Inland temperatures are pleasant in Tanzania because of the high altitude, but along the coast temperatures reach the nineties, and humidity is high. Because Tanzania lies near the equator, the change of seasons does not cause significant variations in temperature.

Flora and Fauna

The contrasts in Tanzania's landscape are illustrated by its varied plant life. On the coast, coconut palms and cashew and banana trees are plentiful. Some of the flora of the interior consists of sparse, dry woodland called miombo. Huge baobab trees grow inland, and their pulp, leaves, and bark are often used for food, medicine, and building materials. The interior also supports regions of thorn trees and lush forests.

On the mountain slopes, thick rainforests start at about 5,000 feet above sea

13

level and include yellowwood and various species of cedar. Around the highest peaks, bamboo and groundsels, which resemble giant cabbages, grow plentifully.

West of the coastal strip and extending about 20 miles inland lies a wilderness of scrub vegetation, dry riverbeds, rocky hills, and giant baobab trees. Overlarge populations of big game and severe dry seasons challenge the delicate balance of nature. Elephants uproot trees to get at the choice top leaves that they cannot reach when the trees are upright. Grasses take the place of the uprooted trees, and, too frequently, fires char the region, forcing nature to start anew.

The Tanzanian government works diligently to balance the population's need for farmland with the animals' need for space in which to roam and breed safely. The national government has established 12 national parks and game preserves where many animals live in their natural surroundings. Streams are inhabited by hippopotamuses and crocodiles, while rhinoceroses, elephants, lions, cheetahs, leopards, giraffes, buffalo, zebras, and ostriches abound on land.

Serengeti National Park covers 5,600 square miles of northern Tanzania and is inhabited by an immense wildlife population, including 1.5 million large game animals. The land varies between treeless savanna—which supports several kinds of grasses and low bushy growth—and thick forest. At times, a quarter of a million

Photo by Phil Porter

The pods on these baobabs will soon bear fruit called monkey bread. Baobabs are not very tall, but their width makes them one of Africa's largest trees.

Tanzania abounds in wildlife. Lions *(above)* rest in the sun, a baboon *(right)* guards her offspring, and flamingos *(below)* wade through a lake.

A narrow road winds down a steep slope onto the floor of Ngorongoro Crater.

gazelles and zebras can be seen moving in long herds toward a new supply of water near the Mbalangeti and Mara rivers.

Ngorongoro Crater—a collapsed volcano —also lies in northern Tanzania. The crater's walls are about 7,000 feet high and 12 miles in diameter. Its floor lies 2,000 feet below the level of the surrounding ground. Home of the largest permanent population of game animals in all of Africa, the crater's residents include lions, cheetahs, and hyenas.

Cities

The largest city and former capital of Tanzania is Dar es Salaam (population 1.1 million). Founded in the 1860s by the sultan of Zanzibar, the city bears an Arabic name that means "haven of peace." The name derives from the sultan's desire to create a refuge for himself away from Zanzibar. Dar es Salaam is on the coast of Tanzania's mainland, just south of Zanzibar Island.

Dar es Salaam is Tanzania's governmental, commercial, and financial center.

Approximately eight million years ago, Ngorongoro was an active volcano whose cone collapsed and formed what is now the largest complete crater in the world.

Although the Arabs and the Germans influenced the development of Dar es Salaam, the capital of Tanzania has maintained a strong African quality.

Home to Arabs, East Indians, and Europeans—although a majority of its residents are African—the city is the crowded hub for much of the country's activity.

In an effort to decentralize various aspects of Tanzanian life, the government chose Dodoma (population 141,000) in 1974 to become the new capital. Centrally located on the Tanzanian mainland, Dodoma gives a focus to the country's large agricultural population. The transfer of government functions to the new capital is taking place gradually and is scheduled to be completed in the early 1990s.

Founded in the fourteenth century by Arab traders, Tanga (population 123,000) is Tanzania's northern deepwater port. The Tanga railway line extends into the country's northern agricultural region. The railway also provides access to the national parks of north central Tanzania.

Residents of Arusha in northeastern Tanzania benefit from a government effort to supply purified water to arid regions.

17

Arusha (population 56,000) is the western endpoint for the Tanga railway and is a tourism and safari center for the region's Serengeti National Park, Mount Kilimanjaro, and Ngorongoro Crater.

Mwanza (population 189,000) lies on the southern shore of Lake Victoria. From Mwanza, boats cross Lake Victoria to Kisumu in Kenya and to Entebbe in Uganda.

Located on Zanzibar Island, the deep-water port of Zanzibar City (population 133,000) displays a mixture of cultures. In what is called "Stone Town," the distinctively Arab influence is seen in the architecture and narrow streets. This section of the city contrasts sharply with Ngambo ("the other side"), largely an African settlement of mud dwellings.

Although elephants do not exist on Zanzibar, the Arabs imported this pointed brass door ornament (used in India to warn elephants away) for decoration.

Photo by Phil Porter

In the late nineteenth century the commercial seaport of Zanzibar City was a starting point for explorers and missionaries to Africa.

Photo by Phil Porter

Olduvai Gorge is the site of a rich fossil bed where anthropologists have unearthed the remains of prehistoric animals and ancestors of the human family.

2) History and Government

The beginning of the known history of Tanzania lies in the Olduvai Gorge. Here, British anthropologists Mary and Louis Leakey found bone fragments, including pieces of skull, and tools. These findings suggest that ancestors of the human family lived in the region 2.3 million years ago. As a result of the Olduvai discoveries, Africa (and Tanzania in particular) is con-

sidered by some to be the original home of humankind.

East Africa, especially Tanzania's mainland and islands, has been explored constantly for more than 2,000 years. Much of Africa's rich and varied history is preserved in its oral tradition as well as in written form. The Arabic language was widely used along Africa's eastern coast,

19

Independent Picture Service

Kondoa, in Dodoma province, is known for its rock paintings dating from the Stone Age. These drawings depict a community engaged in hunting.

and historians have reconstructed much of Tanzania's history from the records of Arab traders. Although the entire story is not yet known, the portion of Africa now known as Tanzania has played a major role in the history of the continent.

Early Migrations

Early migrations of people to the region came from western Africa 3,000 to 5,000 years ago. These immigrants, who are called the Khoikhoi and the San, were hunters and gatherers who spoke languages still found in certain regions of the southern half of Africa. Bantu-speaking people moved into the region from the northwest between 1,500 and 2,000 years ago. These newer immigrants relied on agriculture as well as hunting to support themselves. Unlike the people already settled in the region, they used iron tools.

From the north, groups—such as the Nilotes—came from central Sudan, from the Nile River region, and from the region east of the Nile. They entered mainland Tanzania during the period A.D. 1200 to A.D. 1800. These peoples spoke their own languages but were absorbed by the Bantu-speaking groups. The northerners were cattle herders and farmers. Among them were the people who are known today as the Masai.

Arab Traders

From the tenth to the fifteenth centuries, the coast and islands of East Africa were part of a large Indian Ocean trading area that was dominated by Arab and East Indian merchants. The Arabs were largely from Shiraz, a city located in present-day Iran that controlled the eastern half of the Persian Gulf. Other Arabs came to the region from Oman on the Arabian Peninsula. Merchants also sailed to the coast of the Indian Ocean from the trading center of Delhi, India.

Settlements were established all along the East African coast, and Tanzania had its share of visitors. Kilwa along the southern Tanzanian coast, Bagamoyo farther north, and Zanzibar were among the main

Independent Picture Service

Although they made up only a small fraction of the country's population, the Masai have lived in northern Tanzania for centuries. Many now work in government offices and in private businesses.

trading posts. Ivory and slaves were taken to Arab and East Indian lands by the traders, who traded cloth, iron implements, glass, and decorative items in exchange. Kilwa also controlled the gold trade that came up from the area that is now Mozambique.

These settlements were independent and formed no unified empire. Occasionally, more powerful settlements would extract tribute from weaker ones.

The Arab traders had a less direct impact on interior regions of Tanzania because the terrain there was too difficult for them to settle. The traders did leave their mark, however. The architecture of the coastal and island towns and the Islamic way of life, which guided commercial and social patterns during this period, reflect strong Arab influences. For five centuries the Arabs dominated the coast, and their trading system was well established by the time the first Europeans arrived at the end of the fifteenth century.

Portuguese Influences

At the close of the fifteenth century, Europe was besieged by Islamic invaders who not only were threatening European territory but also were blocking access to the rich markets located in Asia. Looking for alternative trade routes, Vasco da Gama sailed from Portugal around the southern tip of Africa. The explorer's voyage began in 1497, and by 1498

Independent Picture Service

The ruins of this Muslim mosque (house of prayer) near the port of Kilwa exist among many traces of the Portuguese, Arab, and Swahili cultures.

This Portuguese construction was converted into an Arab fort in about 1710.

Photo by Phil Porter

he had reached the East African coast. He observed the prosperous Arab trading settlements, and his reports caused much excitement at the Portuguese court.

Greed for gold, ivory, and slaves, as well as a desire to harm their Islamic enemies, motivated the Portuguese to wage war for control of the East African coast. The trade routes were dominated alternately by the Portuguese and the Arabs, depending on who was victorious in battle during a given year.

By 1698 the Arabs and their allies were able to drive out the Portuguese with a series of counterattacks, and once more the Tanzanian coast came under complete Arab domination. Although some trading posts were destroyed as a result of the conflict between the Arabs and the Portuguese, many of these strongholds were rebuilt and soon thrived again.

Arab Revival

After the Arabs had reestablished control over the coast of East Africa at the end of the seventeenth century, the Arab

Photo by Phil Porter

The "House of Wonders" is the former palace of Sultan Seyyid Said.

pattern of trading and slavery returned. Slaves often were used locally on newly developed plantations, especially on Zanzibar where cloves became a major export. The slave markets of the Middle East and Africa were strong, and many Europeans took part in the slave trade.

One of the most important changes in Arab policy came in 1840, when the capital of the Arabian empire was moved from Muscat, in Oman, to the island of Zanzibar. Zanzibar by this time had become the gateway to trade with the whole coast of East Africa.

The Arab ruler at that time, Sultan Seyyid Said, was courted by the British. They hoped to persuade him to outlaw the slave trade along the East African coast. The British also wanted to curb French influence and to increase legitimate trade. Although the sultan entered into some minor agreements, the slave trade continued.

Said died in 1856, and his sultanate (empire) was divided between his two sons. One son returned to Muscat to control the family holdings in Oman, while the other son remained in Zanzibar to control the East African trade. By 1873 the British were able to convince the sultan of Zanzibar to stop trading (but not to stop owning) slaves by threatening to blockade the island. After the slave trade ended, commerce in cloves, ivory, and rubber increased.

Missionaries

The earliest religious teachers to come to East Africa were Muslims (followers of the Islamic religion). The results of Islamic missionary activity were limited because

This ruin near Tabora was once a house along an Arab trade route where traveling merchants stopped to rest.

Photo by Phil Porter

Members of this Roman Catholic mission in Morogoro purchased slaves in order to release them from bondage.

Europeans Explore the Interior

During the nineteenth century, European interest in the continent of Africa grew stronger after the reports of a new wave of explorers were published. During the next century, East Africa was the scene of frequent European explorations.

New maps and information about East Africa were supplied from the journeys of David Livingstone, Richard Burton, J. H. Speke, and James Grant. Through the work of these travelers, European powers developed an interest in colonizing the area, and East Africa became the arena for international colonial competition.

German Involvement

Germany developed its East African colonial empire largely through the efforts of Carl Peters, head of the Society for German Colonization. In 1884 he made a six-week journey through the interior of the

few Islamic teachers came with the trading ships. The sects represented by the traders were not active in seeking converts. Arab traders knew that conversion of the local peoples to Islam, which forbade one Muslim from enslaving another, would prevent converted Africans from being taken as slaves.

In the 1840s the first groups of Christian missionaries arrived in East Africa from Europe. Their zeal was often diminished by the extremely harsh terrain and by the local diseases that afflicted them. Those who survived set up missions in densely populated areas and concentrated their efforts on converting the elders and local leaders, called chiefs. The missionaries thought that if the chiefs became Christian, the conversion of the rest of the community would follow.

The missionary movement encouraged legitimate forms of commerce, and thus helped to end the slave trade. The missionaries also introduced Western-style education and health practices to the region.

Courtesy of Library of Congress

David Livingstone's writings interested other Europeans in missionary efforts in Tanzania.

24

The German and British colonial governments each claimed a different half of Lake Victoria in the nineteenth century.

mainland and signed a dozen treaties with local leaders. These treaties, of doubtful legality, became the basis for German colonial claims as Europe prepared for the quick division of the continent.

At European conferences, rules were established for colonization, and claims were laid out. As a result of an agreement made with Great Britain, France, and Belgium in 1890, Germany gained control of the regions now known as Rwanda and Burundi as well as mainland Tanzania. Land to the north of the middle of Lake Victoria was to go to the British, and land to the south was to belong to Germany.

All of these plans were made without the help of local African leaders. The partitioning of Africa had profound effects on the distribution of the region's ethnic groups. The division also established international boundaries in places where none had existed before the colonial period.

Bismarck Rocks in Lake Victoria are named after Prince Otto Eduard Leopold von Bismarck, the German statesman who was instrumental in making Tanganyika a German colony.

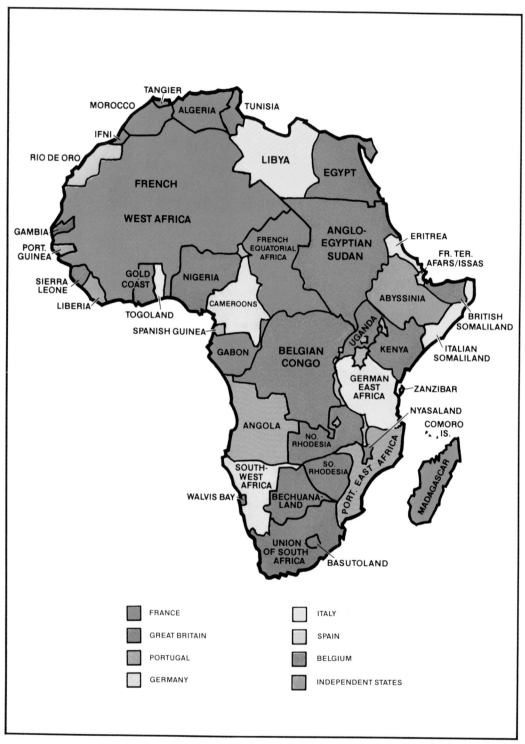

By the late nineteenth century, European powers had carved the continent of Africa into areas of influence. Tanganyika was under the control of Germany as German East Africa, and the British administered Zanzibar. Map information taken from *The Anchor Atlas of World History*, 1978.

Colonial Administration

At first, the German government placed a private firm, the German East Africa Company, in charge of its colonial region. This arrangement failed because the rule of the individual administrators proved to be very harsh. Their policies, particularly concerning private ownership of land and rules requiring men to work as forced laborers, conflicted strongly with local African practices. German concern over the land policy arose when Africans began protesting the division of East Africa into large German-owned plantations. According to African tradition, farmland was worked by the family members of an entire community, and the fruits of their labor were shared.

Finally, in 1891, the German government reasserted control over the colonial administration. Although government officials were no more skillful in administering the colony than private administrators

had been, they had military power at their command that could be used to stop rebellions.

The most famous and largest uprising, the Maji-Maji Revolt (named after a religious ritual meant to protect the African warriors) in 1905, was caused by Germany's forced work policy and its treatment of African workers. The uprising affected the southern half of the colonial region and lasted for two years, costing an estimated 100,000 African lives. The Germans burned hundreds of villages in an attempt to put down the rebellion.

News of the revolt and of the unfair labor conditions that led to it affected the people of Germany. As a result, a new policy protecting African rights was established. German administrators now encouraged African workers to continue their agricultural way of life and no longer forced them to satisfy the labor needs of European planters. Nevertheless, the

Courtesy of American Lutheran Church

Tanzanian farmers, shown here clearing a plot of land, still follow the African tradition of community effort.

Arab slave traders captured Africans from the interior and forced them to travel to the coast, where the captives would be shipped to foreign lands as slaves.

This group of Africans was rescued from an Arab slave ship in the Indian Ocean in 1884.

plantation owners found enough African workers to continue to do the manual labor on colonial properties.

Although the British had stopped the trading of slaves, African slaves still existed in East Africa. The German colonial administration allowed African slaves to buy their freedom after 1901 and decreed that slave-descended children born after 1906 would be free. Slavery was completely abolished after the British gained control of the mainland region following World War I.

Slavery died out slowly on Zanzibar and on the other islands as well, even though they had been under British administration since 1890. Slavery was abolished on the islands by law in 1897, but several provisions within the law made actual freedom for the African slaves unlikely. Progress toward the real end of slavery on the islands was hampered by the Arab need for a labor force. Not until 1911 were the laws that inhibited freedom eliminated. Without jobs or government assistance, however, the newly freed people continued to live in poverty.

British Control

During World War I (1914 to 1918), many Africans died of starvation, and many others died in battle. Little economic production and even less trade took place during these years. In 1919, after the long peace conferences were over, Britain, France, and the United States broke up the German colonial empire. German East Africa, with its poor economy, was not considered ready for self-rule and thus became a protectorate.

In 1922 the international League of Nations chose Britain to administer the former German colony. At this time the mainland region was officially named Tanganyika. The people were governed by indirect rule, meaning that the British used the local African leaders to administer much of the territory. But Africans

Independent Picture Service

Arab slave traders bound their African captives in chains that are now on display in a museum in Bagamoyo, the coastal town from which slaves were shipped to European colonies and Arab countries.

did not want their chiefs to simply become colonial agents, and, when the local leaders were viewed this way, the people did not respond to their leadership.

Agriculture, which had suffered during the war, recovered and surpassed prewar levels. Educational opportunities grew under British supervision, but schools suffered for lack of money during the worldwide depression of the 1930s. In 1929 the African Association was formed as a self-help and social organization, and a branch opened on Zanzibar in 1934.

The British saw Zanzibar as an Arab territory during this period, and the mainland and islands continued to be administered separately. The Arabs extended their clove and coconut plantations on the islands, using Africans as the labor force. Like the Africans, the Shirazis (those who claimed a mixed Arab-and-African heritage) were largely excluded from colonial administration and educational opportunities. The Shirazis formed an association in 1939 to promote their social and economic welfare, though the group did not address political questions. The Arabs and East Indians also formed their own organizations during this time.

World War II and Its Aftermath

During World War II, 80,000 Tanganyikans joined the British forces. They served in North Africa as well as in Madagascar and Burma. The local leaders at home were allowed even more authority during the war, and some alienated themselves further from the people by misusing their power. Because the Japanese dominated the supply of sisal and rubber from southeastern Asia, Britain and its allies relied partially on East African production of these items.

After World War II, Tanganyika became a United Nations (UN) trusteeship under the supervision of Great Britain. This arrangement differed from the mandate established by the League of Nations after World War I in that it encouraged the development of independent political institutions in Tanganyika.

The trusteeship was designed so that the people could become more directly involved in the administration of their own country. Indeed, the goal of the trusteeship was self-government for Tanganyika. To ensure that the trusteeship was working toward this goal, the UN sent visiting missions to Tanganyika every three years to serve as fact-finding groups.

The Tanganyikan African Civil Service Union was organized in the 1920s. Although it did not have much political influence or solidarity, it was one of the first all-African civic organizations. African political power began to develop in 1948 when the African Association split with its Zanzibari branch and became the Tanganyikan African Association (TAA). The TAA focused on local concerns, such as agricultural policies and the way chiefs functioned in the communities.

Photo by Phil Porter

During World War II, the Allies depended on Tanzania's production of sisal, and today the nation is a leading producer of the plant. Sisal fibers taken from the plant's inner bark are used to make coarse materials and rope.

In 1956 Julius Nyerere spoke at a hearing before the General Assembly's Trusteeship Committee of the United Nations. As president of the Tanganyikan African National Union (TANU), Nyerere petitioned in his speech for Tanganyika's independence.

In the first two decades of its history, the TAA gained little public support and had only a minor effect on political events in Tanganyika. In 1953, however, the TAA elected a young schoolteacher named Julius Nyerere as its president, and he set about reforming the organization. Under his leadership, a new constitution for the party was drafted, and the organization's name was changed to the Tanganyikan African National Union (TANU). Nyerere hoped to gain recognition for the party among a majority of Africans, not just among a small, educated group. The goals of TANU included agricultural reform and free elections.

Meanwhile, in the 1950s, the British authorities in Tanganyika started their own campaign, which was directed against TANU and its leaders. The British were attempting to encourage local associations rather than a national, political organization. Chiefs were bribed to turn their people away from TANU. British authorities refused to issue licenses for public meetings and rallies supported by TANU. Discrimination against those who were active in the party prevented them from being hired by government bureaus. TANU was outlawed in certain districts as a threat to law and order.

The party overcame these obstacles with the help of trade union members and the repeated visits of the UN mission in charge of the trusteeship in Tanganyika. TANU held meetings, at times secretly, and distributed literature around the country despite the colonial government's ban on the party.

Julius Nyerere and TANU

Julius Nyerere and the leaders of TANU presented their case to the UN mission in 1954. The party leadership pointed out that poverty and illiteracy hampered Tanganyika's economic and social progress.

The UN mission, after studying the situation, proposed a schedule for independence targeted for 1975. Tanganyika's

31

President Nyerere's policy included self-reliance for Tanzania. "TANU," he said in the 1960s, "is involved in a war against poverty and oppression . . . We now intend to bring about a revolution which will ensure that we are never again victims of these things."

colonial administration responded by trying to downplay TANU's importance. To maintain the support of the UN mission, Julius Nyerere flew to New York to speak before the UN General Assembly. Nyerere demanded free elections and increased African participation in the government of the trusteeship. He impressed many UN members with his moderate policies. He promised, for example, full citizenship and participation for Asians and Europeans living in Tanganyika after independence.

The colonial government tried to lessen TANU's popularity by sponsoring the United Tanganyika party (UTP). The UTP proposed that, until independence, Tanganyika should be the responsibility of Britain, not the United Nations. But the UTP gained few members.

TANU, on the other hand, could count on 250,000 supporters. In the 1958–1959 elections for the Legislative Council (a law-making body with limited power), TANU demonstrated its influence by gaining a majority in several provinces and, a year later, by winning a dozen more seats. After the elections, the UTP disbanded because it had become clear that TANU had wider popular support.

Events Leading to Independence

Simultaneous with the growth of TANU as a political power was a change in the top leadership of the trusteeship. The new colonial governor of Tanganyika, Sir Richard Turnbull, had been chief secretary during a period of violence in Kenya in the 1950s. His experience in Kenya made him resolve to prevent similar events in Tanganyika. Julius Nyerere welcomed Turnbull's appointment to Tanganyika because Nyerere felt that the new colonial administration would be more liberal toward TANU and its quest for self-government.

After the elections of 1958–1959, the hope of independence prompted members of TANU to cooperate with colonial authorities. In late 1959 Nyerere predicted independence within five years. Governor Turnbull created great excitement when he announced in December 1959 that Tanganyika would have some sort of responsible self-government within the following year.

The last UN mission came to Tanganyika in 1960. After exchanging letters with the colonial authorities and with Julius Nyerere, the mission reported that the country would achieve its independence as early as possible despite the serious economic problems that Tanganyika faced.

After TANU won another election in 1960, Governor Turnbull asked Julius Nyerere to form a government. The British convened a constitutional conference in London in March 1961. The constitution was drawn up based on the British model, calling for a parliament, prime minister, and cabinet. The new constitution guaranteed impartial law courts and the right of all adults to vote.

Under Nyerere's leadership, the emerging nation focused on developing educational programs, increasing agricultural productivity, and fostering African unity. Equality was a particular concern of Nyerere's, not only for black Africans who were now coming to political power but also for the Arab, European, and East Indian minorities. Nyerere also took a strong stand against apartheid—racial separateness—in the nation of South Africa. He appealed to all independent African nations to boycott products from South Africa until apartheid policies were dropped.

Self-Government and Independence

Tanganyika achieved self-government on May 1, 1961, and complete independence came in December of that year. At first, Tanganyikans supervised their own affairs under the guidance of the British governor, who still had the power to make decisions affecting foreign affairs and defense. Full independence meant that Tanganyika was freed entirely from colonial administration. In the first independent government of Tanganyika, Julius Nyerere held the office of prime minister. The Legislative Council—a historic symbol of colonial rule—was replaced by a national assembly.

Nyerere encouraged European settlers to continue to live and work in independent Tanganyika. He did not want these wealthy and highly trained people to leave the new nation. Although the announced policy and goal of the government was to replace European government workers with Africans, Nyerere assured the Europeans that they would not be replaced until they retired or left of their own choice.

Independent Picture Service

A climber placed Tanganyika's flag and a symbolic torch of freedom at the top of Mount Kilimanjaro to celebrate independence in 1961.

33

On Queen's Day in October 1961, two months before Tanganyika achieved full independence, Governor Turnbull *(left)* inspected troops. A band *(below)* participates in Queen's Day ceremonies.

Photo by Phil Porter

Photo by Phil Porter

Zanzibar's Road to Independence

In contrast to the relatively peaceful independence movement in Tanganyika, Zanzibar had a stormy road to self-rule because its people were divided along ethnic and cultural lines. One of the major groups in Zanzibar was the Shirazis—who claimed to be the mixed descendants of Africans and of Persian Arabs, who began arriving in Zanzibar as far back as the tenth century. Another group consisted of Africans of mainland ancestry. Nevertheless, the most powerful people in Zanzibar were the Arabs, who lived in the cities and who had collected great wealth through trade. A small East Indian community engaged mainly in commerce and finance also lived on the island. Each group distrusted the others.

These groups began to develop political parties. The British colonial government continued to see Zanzibar and the other islands as an Arab state. To prevent Arab domination when national independence arrived, Africans and Shirazis joined to form what finally became the Afro-Shirazi party (ASP). The Arabs organized into the Zanzibar Nationalist party (ZNP).

The British faced increasing opposition in the period after World War II, not only from the Africans and Shirazis of Zanzibar but from the Arabs as well. Under British administration, Arabs had ruled Zanzibar through the power of the sultanate. But in 1954, as the Arabs began to maneuver for independent control of the island, they started a boycott against the British colonial government.

Several elections to the Zanzibari Legislative Council were held in the 1950s, and the Afro-Shirazi coalition won widespread public support. The ZNP used its broader

Zanzibaris do their daily marketing and other errands in an Indian section of the island. The various ethnic groups safeguard portions of their cultural identity in their own communities.

Photo by Phil Porter

Objects in the Zanzibar Museum serve as reminders of Arab influence on the history of the island.

The traditional Arab dhow, common to the East African coast, has been a model for many sailing vessels over the centuries.

Tanzania requires a period of service to the nation from its young people. These women parade as members of the National Service, which trains them in agricultural and industrial improvement programs.

political expertise to extend Arab control in later elections. By the time of the pre-independence election in July 1963, the Arabs and their political allies were able to win a majority of the legislative seats even though the ASP won 54 percent of the popular vote.

Zanzibar gained its independence from Great Britain on December 10, 1963. Independence intensified the problems on Zanzibar and the other islands, however, and two months later Zanzibar was the scene of a violent coup d'état. The ASP overthrew Sultan Seyyid Khalifa and the ZNP leadership, and Abeid Amani Karume, head of the ASP, became the leader of Zanzibar.

Tanganyika and Zanzibar Unite

The governments of the world were surprised when Tanganyika and Zanzibar joined together in 1964 to form the United Republic of Tanzania. But to people who knew East African history, the union was less surprising, since Zanzibar had long been the gateway to the mainland.

Nyerere realized that Zanzibar was in fragile condition because its life as a nation began with much tension and internal division. Tanganyika and Zanzibar allied into one nation to protect themselves and each other from the instability that threatened Zanzibar. TANU and the ASP, which already had political ties with each other, joined to become the Chama Cha Mapinduzi (CCM), or Revolutionary party.

Nyerere was the president of the new republic. Karume, who retained the title of president of Zanzibar, was also the first vice president of Tanzania. The National Assembly was expanded to include a large Zanzibari representation, and the ratio

37

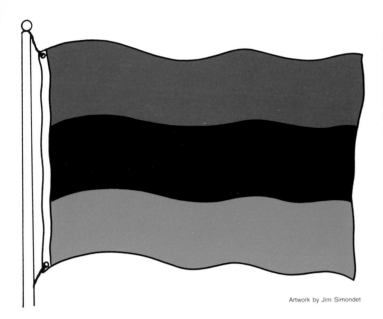

In February 1964 Zanzibar's flag consisted of three colored horizontal bands and one white vertical stripe. Blue represented the sea around the islands; black stood for the Zanzibaris; green symbolized the land; and white signified peace and harmony.

Artwork by Jim Simondet

of island-to-mainland government officials was decreed by law.

In 1972 Karume was assassinated. His governing of Zanzibari affairs had been harsh, especially toward the Arab minority who eventually carried out his assassination. President Nyerere appointed Aboud Jumbe to succeed Karume as president of Zanzibar and as a vice president of Tanzania. The prosecution of Karume's assassins closed the most unstable chapter of Zanzibar's recent history. Since then, relations among Zanzibar's ethnic groups have been smoother, and the union of islanders with mainlanders has strengthened.

Conflict with Uganda

In 1971 Tanzania entered a decade of conflict with its neighbor to the north. Ugan-

After Tanganyika gained its independence in 1961, it added two gold stripes to its former colonial flag.

Artwork by Jim Simondet

dan general Idi Amin overthrew Uganda's president Milton Obote and installed himself as the country's leader. Nyerere was among the first outsiders to condemn the brutal nature of the Amin regime.

Obote operated in exile from Dar es Salaam. In 1972 Obote and his supporters unsuccessfully tried to regain Uganda by military action, staging their attack from Tanzanian territory. Although Nyerere wanted to refrain from fighting with Uganda directly, military conflict between the countries became more and more likely.

After Uganda occupied a portion of Tanzanian territory along their mutual border in 1978, Tanzania launched an invasion in 1979 with 20,000 of its troops. The Tanzanian forces, along with 1,200 Ugandan exiles, captured Uganda's capital city of Kampala. Tanzania occupied a large portion of Uganda until 1981, when elections were held and Obote resumed the presidency.

Tanzania's Political Development

After achieving independence, Tanzania pursued a policy of African socialism. A large-scale attempt to transfer traditional patterns of village cooperation to the

Residents of Kampala, Uganda, celebrate the overthrow of the Idi Amin government by the exiled Ugandan and the Tanzanian forces in April 1979.

national level, African socialism stresses shared labor and equality. According to this idea, working together will lead the people of Tanzania to become an extended family. This notion is embodied in the movement's motto, *Ujamaa*, meaning "togetherness" or "familyhood."

Nyerere also developed a concept of African national democracy, which emphasizes discussion until consensus, or general agreement, is reached. In Tanzania—as in many other African nations—discussions take place within a one-party system. Therefore, dissent is allowed within the party during discussions, but, after consensus is reached, decisions are announced with a unified voice.

In the 1960s, 1970s, and early 1980s, Tanzania supported independence movements in Angola, Mozambique, and Southern Rhodesia (now Zimbabwe), as they struggled against their colonial administrations. Tanzania continues to actively speak out against apartheid by assisting the outlawed African National Congress of South Africa. Tanzania is also a leading member in the Organization for African Unity (OAU). The OAU brings together the independent nations of Africa to attempt to solve hostile disputes, to develop programs for economic development, and to encourage cultural, scientific, and educational exchanges.

In 1985, at age 63, Nyerere stepped down from the presidency and began to travel through the country as head of the CCM. Ali Hassan Mwinyi, a Muslim Zanzibari, was elected to the presidency. Known as a politician who focuses on the practical, Mwinyi is working alongside party leader Nyerere to improve economic life in Tanzania.

Independent Picture Service

Schoolchildren practice the policy of *ujamaa* (togetherness) by helping to make bricks for a new hospital building in the Shinyanga region.

The activities that take place in these government buildings in Dar es Salaam will be completely transferred to Dodoma by 1992, when it officially becomes Tanzania's capital city.

Government

The United Republic of Tanzania has an executive branch composed of a president and two vice presidents. The president is elected by the voters and, in turn, selects the other two executive officers from the members of the National Assembly.

The first vice president's duties include serving as prime minister of the National Assembly, Tanzania's unicameral (one-house) law-making body. This legislative branch of the government has over 200 members, and approximately one-fourth of the seats are reserved for representatives from the islands. The second vice president serves as head of the local political party of the islands.

Mainland Tanzania is divided into 17 provinces, each of which is governed by a commissioner. The islands of Zanzibar and Pemba are divided into three administrative areas. Regional commissioners are appointed by the central government to oversee the activities in each region.

Tanzania's youth believe that their government will continue to work for improved social and economic conditions.

3) The People

Tanzania's population growth rate is 3.1 percent, which means that the population may double in 20 years. The population in 1987 was 23.5 million, with 18 percent of the people living in urban areas. Tanzania hosts several cultures, and many members of Tanzania's ethnic groups intermarry. Though important, ethnic loyalties are not central to national life. Family ties, however, are significant, and families gather to commemorate births, marriages, and deaths, as well as to celebrate good harvests. The people of Tanzania are primarily African in ethnic origin, with people of non-African heritage accounting for only 1 percent of the population.

Tanzanians work predominantly in agriculture, and a majority of them live in rural areas.

A traditional feature of Masai culture is the group's colorful clothing and ornate jewelry.

Ethnic Mixture

The coastal countries of East Africa are the home of many cultural groups of Asian, European, and African origin. Bantu-speaking communities migrated into present-day Tanzania during the first millenia (1,000 years) A.D., and Arabic-speaking peoples from the Persian Gulf and Oman settled along the coast. Many of the Arabs intermarried with the Bantu-speaking peoples, and gradually the Swahili culture and language emerged as a blend of these two groups.

South Asian immigration—from India and Pakistan to the mainland—began at the beginning of the twentieth century when workers were needed to build railways from the coast to the interior. Descendants of these railway employees frequently are merchants, technicians, and financial managers.

Thousands of Europeans came to Tanzania during the first half of the twentieth century and settled in the area's fertile lands. Some now occupy positions in private business or work as civil servants in schools and government offices.

African Ethnic Groups

The African population embraces more than 120 ethnic groups and cultures, although many are quite small. Most Tanzanians live in rural areas; about one-fifth of the nation's population is urbanized. Many of these rural people speak Kiswahili in addition to English and the tongue of their individual ethnic group.

The Chaga and Masai live near Mount Kilimanjaro, where the countryside is fertile and gets plenty of rainfall. The Chaga are of Bantu origin and live in one of the

Independent Picture Service

With long-leafed banana trees towering in the background, a leader watches with interest as the Wanyakyusa celebrate their harvest by dancing.

In Moshi, a town at the foot of Mount Kilimanjaro, the Chaga pick berries that contain coffee beans.

Independent Picture Service

This Sambaa man lives in eastern Tanzania and speaks a Bantu dialect.

Independent Picture Service

most densely populated areas of Tanzania. Their coffee-growing cooperatives thrive, and many Chaga are successful business and professional people.

The Masai are well known throughout the world. Their military strength was respected by explorers during the nineteenth century, and their land was rarely disturbed. Masai villages are often temporary, because the group moves on when their herds require fresh grazing land. The Masai inhabit a sparsely populated plain

Independent Picture Service

Two Wagogo women from central Tanzania hoe the land with a widely used tool called a *jembe.*

Independent Picture Service

Zanzibari children sit alongside a door carved with intricate patterns that are traditional in Arab culture.

Tanzania's infant mortality rate (111 deaths per 1,000 births) and life expectancy (52 years) are average for Africa but are worse than figures for Europe and North America.

west of Kilimanjaro that extends north into Kenya.

In the central highlands the population remains small but stable in spite of the country's overall population increase. Here, the largest ethnic groups are the Sukuma, who are subsistence farmers and cotton producers, and the Nyamwezi, who have become known as traders in addition to being small-scale farmers. The population in the region is sparse because few rivers originate in the dry forests, and many crop-destroying insects thrive. Most settlements consist of only a few houses, while a large village may have as many as 100 houses.

The coastal, Kiswahili-speaking people live in cities and villages on the mainland and on nearby islands and represent a variety of ethnic backgrounds. Most Swa-

hilis are followers of Islam, the religion founded by the prophet Muhammad in the Middle East during the seventh century. Other groups came to the coastal region from the African interior or from Asia and eventually blended into the Swahili culture.

Languages

The government of Tanzania adopted Kiswahili, a mixture of Arabic and Bantu, as its official language in 1967. Bantu words represent about two-thirds of the Kiswahili vocabulary, and most of the remaining one-third are of Arabic origin. Some German and English words have been introduced into Kiswahili in the twentieth century. For example, *shule* is the Kiswahili word for school and is nearly the same as the German word *schule*, and *motakaa* is the equivalent of motor car in English. Scholars also have noted Kiswahili's connection to Persian, Hindi, and Turkish.

Originally written in Arabic, Kiswahili is now written in the Latin alphabet, and Arabic characters are used only for ceremonial documents. As a spoken language, Kiswahili spread along the trade routes. Millions of people living as far west as Burundi and Zaire and as far south as Zambia use Kiswahili as a form of communication.

There are ethnic groups in northern Tanzania, near Arusha, who speak Nilotic. This family of languages is generally associated with the cattle-herding people who originated along the Nile River Valley. A few thousand other Tanzanians speak a form of "click" language, which is made with special clicking sounds. Clicking is a distinctive characteristic of some of the major languages of southern Africa.

Health

Tanzania has made health care a top national priority since independence in 1964. Life expectancy has risen from 38 to 52

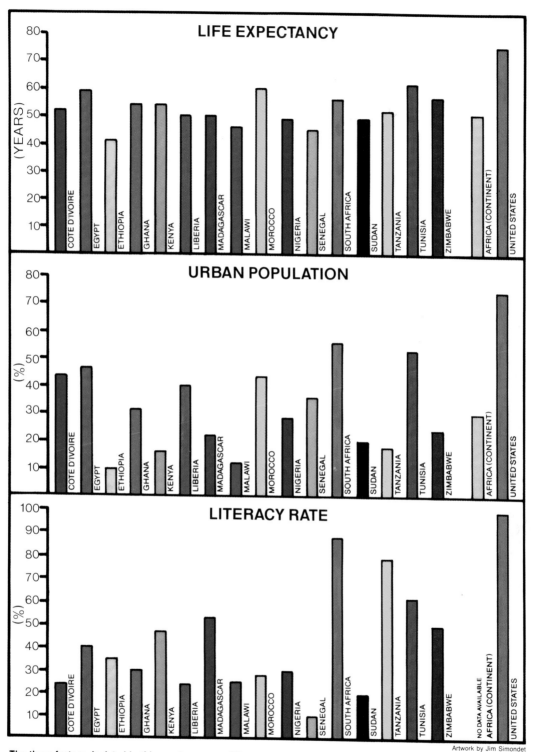

The three factors depicted in this graph suggest differences in the quality of life among 16 African nations. Averages for the United States and the entire continent of Africa are included for comparison. Data taken from "1987 World Population Data Sheet" and *PC-Globe*.

These men are playing *bao,* a challenging game of wits that originated in Iran.

years. (The life expectancy for Africa as a whole is 51 years.) The infant mortality rate is estimated at 111 deaths for every 1,000 children under one year of age. This figure is near the average infant mortality rate in Africa.

The government of Tanzania is building hospitals and clinics for people in remote rural areas. Medicines and nutritional supplements are being distributed to help fight the major diseases—tuberculosis, malaria, dysentery, schistosomiasis (caused by parasites attacking the intestines), elephantiasis (a skin disease), smallpox, and typhoid. Sleeping sickness is a widespread disease transmitted by tsetse flies, which inhabit large regions of Tanzania.

The people of Central and East Africa have a very serious problem with acquired immune deficiency syndrome (AIDS). Accurate methods for reporting this disease are still developing, but Tanzania registered 1,130 cases of AIDS with the World Health Organization (WHO) in 1987.

AIDS researchers estimate that five million Africans, including a relatively large proportion of Tanzanians, already carry the virus that causes the disease.

The government is striving to increase the number of physicians as well as the number of available hospital beds. With 82 percent of the population living in rural areas, health care is expensive because transportation costs are high and because electricity for refrigerating drugs is difficult to provide. Furthermore, less than half of the population has access to pure drinking water.

Education

Education is one of the biggest items in the national budget. Julius Nyerere was the first Tanzanian to become a university graduate, and he has emphasized education from the nation's very beginning. Between 1975 and 1983, for example, the percentage of children enrolled in elementary schools increased from 53 to 87 percent. Primary schools offer instruction in history, geography, mathematics, health education, physical education, and science. Classes are conducted in Kiswahili, as well as in English. Tanzania's overall literacy rate is 79 percent.

The university at Dar es Salaam offers courses in engineering, education, medicine, business, agriculture, and forestry. The Institute for Kiswahili Research provides academic opportunities for language scholars and professors of literature to understand the history of Tanzania's peoples. Over a dozen teachers' colleges, as well as many secondary and technical schools, are well established in Tanzania.

Religion

With its varied colonial background, Tanzania also has a long history of both Islam and Christianity. Of Tanzanians, 35 percent hold Christian beliefs, and 35 percent are of the Islamic faith. Thirty percent follow the same traditional African beliefs that the first Islamic and Christian missionaries found when they arrived. These original beliefs include an acknowledgment of a supreme being, a reverence for one's ancestors, and a recognition of the connection between nature and spirit.

Independent Picture Service

Muslim women, each wearing a *buibui* (a long black garment worn for modesty), pass an old Arab building in Zanzibar City.

On the islands, the large majority of the people are Muslims. On the mainland, Roman Catholics make up the largest Christian denomination, with 18 percent of the population. Episcopalians and Lutherans are also heavily represented in the Christian population.

Photo by Phil Porter

The University of Dar es Salaam is Tanzania's national university. Tanzania maintains several colleges, although only a small portion of the education budget is spent on higher education.

Photo by Phil Porter

Students compete in the high jump at a secondary school in Tabora.

Courtesy of Janet Stanley, Eliot Elisofon Archives, National Museum of African Art, Smithsonian Institution

An Anglican church has replaced the slave market that once prospered on this site.

Photo by Phil Porter

Women plant sweet potatoes in an ujamaa village.

4) The Economy

Agriculture

During the colonial period, the Germans and the British built fewer roads and railways and developed less industry in mainland Tanzania than they did in other areas of East Africa. Moreover, the export trade was not as highly developed as it was in Zanzibar or other parts of the region. The newly independent government inherited these conditions in 1964. It set out to improve the country's economic situation with plans for modernization and nationalization (changing businesses from private ownership to government control).

Tanzania is primarily an agricultural country. Tanzanians provide most of their own food by growing rice, cassavas, papayas, wheat, sweet potatoes, maize (corn), sugar, and bananas on small farms that dot the countryside. These domestic products are not exported, however, because Tanzania is not self-sufficient in foodstuffs.

Significant changes, such as the introduction of chemical fertilizers, have modernized the agricultural methods used by Tanzanian farmers since the early 1960s.

Some farmers sell cotton, a leading crop, to government cooperatives. These women are carrying the raw material to a cooperative market on Ukerewe Island in Lake Victoria.

After coffee beans have been extracted from their berries, workers spread them out to dry in the tropical sun.

Picking tea is a painstaking task that requires the work of many harvesters.

Coffee, Tanzania's leading export, is often grown on plantations or on cooperative farms.

Fertilizers and other petroleum-based products, however, become less accessible to individual farmers, as well as to farming cooperatives, as oil becomes more costly.

Most Tanzanian farms are small and are worked by hand with simple tools. Frequently, women do more farm labor than men do because women remain in the countryside while men work in the towns and cities.

The government of Tanzania encourages farmers to work together to develop cooperative farms. The government believes that cooperatives will increase agricultural output through mechanization, cooperative purchasing of seeds and fertilizers, and cooperative selling.

MAIN CROPS

In addition to developing the farm economy in order to better feed the nation's people, Tanzania also is striving to produce cash crops that will provide the income essential to economic growth. In 1984 Tanzania's leading exports were coffee, cotton, and tea. Coffee accounted for $187 million in export revenues, cotton produced $50 million, and tea brought in $28 million. These products were followed in export income by spices, tobacco, and sisal (a fiber used to make rope).

The rich coffee of Tanzania is quite popular in Europe, Asia, and the United States. One of Tanzania's most valuable cash crops, coffee is grown largely in the northern mountains. Many farmers have small holdings and sell their crop through the national coffee cooperative. The northern coffee plantations are owned by Europeans and Asians, who employ Tanzanians to grow and harvest the crop.

Cotton, the second most important export, is grown along the coast and in the plateau regions up to 4,000 feet above sea level, as well as in areas around Lake Victoria. Almost all of Tanzania's cotton is cultivated on small farms and is sold through cooperatives. Foreign investors, on the other hand, raise tea on large acreages. Grown mainly in the southern highlands and in the northeastern mountains near Tanga, the tea is marketed in London, England, or in Nairobi, Kenya.

LIVESTOCK

In regions where rainfall is scarce and where crops are difficult to cultivate, Tanzanians have turned to cattle raising. In traditional African communities, cattle are considered a measure of a family's wealth and prestige.

Zebus are a measurement of a Tanzanian's wealth. In addition to being raised as livestock, these cattle are beasts of burden in the country's largely agricultural economy.

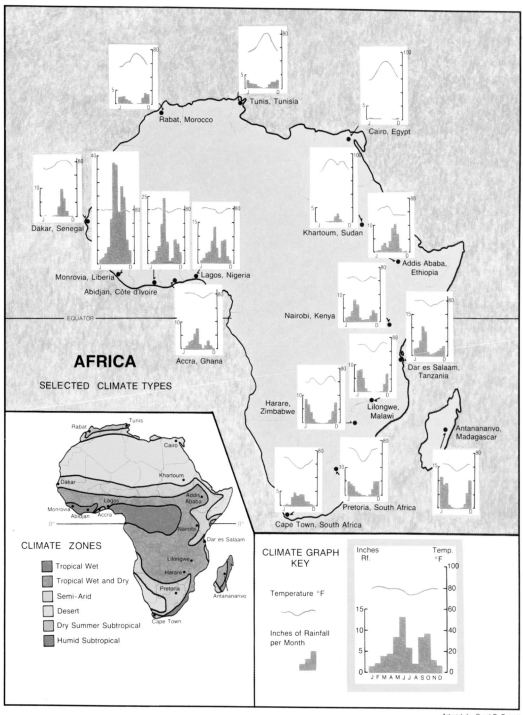

AFRICA

SELECTED CLIMATE TYPES

Rabat, Morocco

Tunis, Tunisia

Cairo, Egypt

Dakar, Senegal

Monrovia, Liberia

Abidjan, Côte d'Ivoire

Lagos, Nigeria

Khartoum, Sudan

Addis Ababa, Ethiopia

EQUATOR

Accra, Ghana

Nairobi, Kenya

Dar es Salaam, Tanzania

Harare, Zimbabwe

Lilongwe, Malawi

Antananarivo, Madagascar

Pretoria, South Africa

Cape Town, South Africa

CLIMATE ZONES

Rabat
Tunis
Cairo
Khartoum
Dakar
Lagos
Monrovia
Abidjan   Accra
Addis Ababa
0°
Nairobi
Dar es Salaam
Lilongwe
Harare
Pretoria
Antananarivo
Cape Town

- Tropical Wet
- Tropical Wet and Dry
- Semi-Arid
- Desert
- Dry Summer Subtropical
- Humid Subtropical

CLIMATE GRAPH KEY

Inches Rf.

Temp. °F

Temperature °F

Inches of Rainfall per Month

J F M A M J J A S O N D

Artwork by Carol F. Barrett

These climate graphs show the monthly changes in the average rainfall received and in the average temperature from January to December for the capital cities of 16 African nations. Dar es Salaam, Tanzania, is fairly typical of a tropical wet and dry climate. The city receives about 40 inches of rainfall each year, with the dry season occurring in June, July, and August. Data taken from *World-Climates* by Willy Rudloff, Stuttgart, 1981.

55

Acres of tobacco grow on this farm in the Tabora region of western Tanzania.

Goats and sheep contribute to the domestic meat supply.

The most common breed of livestock is the humped zebu, a small, short-horned variety of cattle. Ranchers near Lake Victoria raise a long-horned breed called the ankole. In addition to cattle, Tanzanians are extensively involved in raising sheep, goats, and donkeys. Chickens are common in Tanzania but are considered a special food and are often eaten at holiday time or on other special occasions.

Mineral Wealth

Poor roads have slowed development of the country's mineral wealth. The most developed mining sites are in Tanzania's gem and industrial diamond industries. Accounting for three-fourths of the nation's mineral income, diamonds have been mined since 1940 in western Tanzania and

Independent Picture Service

In 1940 Tanzanians discovered diamonds near Shinyanga in what became known as the Mwadui diamond mines. The remainder of Tanzania's leading mineral export may be depleted by the 1990s, although the government continues to search for new deposits.

Independent Picture Service

Young Tanzanians who live on the coast shell cashews for their parents. When the children are finished, their father will bag the nuts and then will market them.

57

In the early 1970s the United States sponsored a rock-crushing plant in Tanzania to help build the Tan-Zam Highway, a road that links the port of Dar es Salaam with Zambia's copper mines.

around the port of Mwanza. Some of the diamonds are of gem quality, and the rest are used for industrial purposes. The largest Tanzanian diamond mined so far weighs slightly over 240 carats (1.7 ounces). The Tanzanian government owns 50 percent of the diamond industry; British investors own the other half.

Secondary minerals mined in Tanzania include gold, tanzanite (a blue gemstone), salt, tin, and mica (a thin, transparent metal). Gold is particularly important, accounting for nearly 15 percent of Tanzania's mining income. Good evidence exists that oil reserves are present in Tanzania. If these reserves become accessible, much of the country's export earnings—now used to pay for foreign oil—could be used to help solve the nation's economic and social problems.

Industry

Industrial development has been slow in Tanzania. Lacking substantial investment capital since the colonial period, Tanzania is now trying to establish new industries. In the 1970s the textile industry, based on the nation's production of cotton, became profitable for Tanzania because processing and manufacturing occurred within the country rather than overseas. Textiles, clothing, and raw cotton are sold extensively abroad.

In an effort to become self-reliant and to gain broader control over its economic life,

Tanzania's climate is suitable for the cultivation of cotton, and large amounts of the fiber are used in the country's textile industry.

The harbor at Dar es Salaam is busy with fishing boats, recreational vehicles, and ships carrying goods to and from Tanzania.

Tanzania nationalized many industries in the early 1970s. The government negotiated with the owners of the companies, reached an agreement on the amount of money the government would pay in compensation, and then took control of these firms. Since 1977, however, the government has encouraged private investment once again. It particularly welcomes private investment in small companies that will provide essential goods for Tanzanians to use.

Forestry

Over 13 percent of Tanzania is covered by trees. Most of the forests are open woodland, but some dense forests exist in small areas. The trees are valuable as a raw export material and as a means to stop soil erosion caused by flooding.

A woman carries firewood alongside the railway that runs from Dar es Salaam to Mwanza.

Generally, the forests are situated at high altitudes in northern and northeastern Tanzania, where rainfall is plentiful. Southwestern Tanzania also contains important areas of standing timber, and most of the coastal region is covered with mangrove forests. The principal timbers cut for commercial use are mahogany, cedar, blackwood, and camphorwood. Since 1920 the government has managed the forests and constantly improves their use and conservation.

Transportation

The Tanzanian government—in cooperation with the Zambian government and the People's Republic of China—constructed a 1,116-mile-long railway line that links the copper-producing country of Zambia to the seaport of Dar es Salaam. Chinese technicians and engineers joined Tanzanians to survey the land, prepare the railbed, lay the track, and build service areas along the railway. Completed in 1974, the railroad is a vital overland connection, especially for Zambia, whose other rail routes to the sea were cut off during the wars of independence in Angola and Zimbabwe.

Workers in the cities usually travel to and from work by foot, bicycle, or bus. Buses connect all the major cities and towns and serve most of the rural areas. The major cities also are served by Air Tanzania, British Airways, and other major airlines, and smaller aircraft leave daily from Dar es Salaam for the large national game parks and tourist centers.

Zanzibar's Economy

Zanzibar, like the mainland, has a predominantly agricultural economy. The islands of Zanzibar and Pemba have earned the nickname "the Islands of Cloves" because they produce the majority of the world's cloves and clove oil.

The clove industry in Zanzibar dates back to the 1830s, when the island served

Zanzibaris make several products from coconut palms. The nuts, when green, yield a drinkable liquid; the white, nutty material inside can be eaten fresh or dried; the sun-dried white material—called copra—makes coconut oil; and the leaves can be used to make roofing for village homes.

Photo by Phil Porter

as a base for Arab activity in East Africa. Sultan Seyyid Said from Oman introduced the spice to the island, and in less than 75 years the clove plantations of Zanzibar were producing about three-fourths of the world's supply.

Cloves come from the dried flower bud of a tropical tree and are used in the preparation of food around the world. The spice is also an important ingredient in the production of cigarettes in southern Asia, and many of Tanzania's cloves are exported to that region. Cloves and other spices grown on the Indian Ocean islands are the nation's fourth largest export, and they are Zanzibar's main agricultural product.

Other Zanzibari exports include coconuts and copra. Copra, the dried meat of the coconut, is the source of coconut oil, which is often used in making soap. The local government of Zanzibar has tried to introduce a variety of crops and has encouraged growing rice for local use. Zanzibar is also famous for its seashells, pottery, jewelry, rope, and mats.

Photo by Susanne Derby

A woman prepares coconuts for cooking. Grated coconut forms the base of many Tanzanian dishes.

Photo by Phil Porter

Clove seeds grow on a plantation in Zanzibar. It is the dried buds—and not the seeds—that are picked and used as a spice.

Tourism

Tourism is an important source of income for Tanzania. The Tanzania Tourist Corporation (TTC) was formed in 1977 to encourage and develop this sector of the economy. Tanzania is rich in natural beauty, and its national parks are popular. Serengeti National Park, Ngorongoro Crater, Mount Kilimanjaro, Olduvai Gorge, Lake Victoria, and Lake Tanganyika are among the destinations of many foreign visitors each year.

Tourists take special interest in Tanzanian arts, especially carvings made of ebony and ivory. The carvings may convey traditional religious themes, capture the natural beauty of the countryside, or express Tanzanian humor.

From a treetop, storks overlook Serengeti National Park, a major tourist attraction in Tanzania that covers 5,600 square miles of savanna (grassland).

Photo by Phil Porter

The Future

Tanzania faces many economic obstacles. In the 1980s food production fell, and the export of cash crops also decreased. At the same time, industrial production in the country declined. The Ugandan war, drought, and climbing oil prices have contributed to the nation's economic difficulties.

Although they are among the poorest people of Africa, Tanzanians are committed to solving their economic problems. Focusing on the village level, the government is making changes in land use and in land-holding policies, hoping that a better agricultural output will result.

Despite its problems, Tanzania is politically stable in a region that has been marked by instability. It continues to work toward African unity and to maintain its nonalignment policy. Tanzania's path of African socialism is geared to face the challenges of the future, and the nation's people and its leaders are ready to follow the course.

Courtesy of Agency for International Development

The success of Tanzania's agriculture will rely partially on graduates of the Morogoro Agricultural College.

Photo by Phil Porter

Because government efforts are aimed at improving village conditions, this young herder can anticipate completing at least a secondary school education.

Index